Knowing God Intimately

Dennis Burke, Ph.D.

Dedication

To my wife for her patience, her labor, her ideas, and her inspiration toward this manuscript.

Thank you, Vikki, for being my co-laborer in ministry and my companion in life.

Unless otherwise stated all Scripture quotations are taken from the *New King James Version* of the Bible.

The Amplified Bible, New Testament (AMP). 1954, 1958 by the Lockman Foundation, La Habra, California. *The Amplified Bible, Old Testament* (AMP). 1962, 1964 by Zondervan Publishing House Grand Rapids, Michigan.

The Bible, A New Translation. 1950, 1952, 1953, 1954 by James A.R. Moffatt. Harper & Row, Publishers, Inc., New York, New York.

The Modern Language Bible, The New Berkeley Version in Modern English (MLB), Rev. Ed. 1945, 1959, 1969 by Zondervan Publishing House, Grand Rapids, Michigan.

New American Standard Bible (NAS). 1960, 1962, 1963, 1968, 1971, 1972, 1973, 1975, 1977 by The Lockman Foundation, La Habra, California.

The New Testament in Modern English (Phillips), Rev. Ed. 1958, 1960, 1972 by J.B. Phillips. The Macmillam Publishing Co., Inc., New York, New York.

New Testament in Modern Speech (Weymouth) by Richard Francis Weymouth. 1978 by Kregel Publication, Grand Rapids, Michigan.

The Twentieth Century New Testament. Moody Bible Institute, Chicago, Illinois.

Knowing God Intimately
ISBN 978-0-89274-349-0
© 1985 by Dennis Burke

Dennis Burke Ministries
PO Box 150043, Arlington, TX 76015

Table of Contents

CHAPTER 1

Knowing God Intimately

The knowledge of God, who He is and what pleases Him, is the longing of every true believer. Throughout the Word of God, it is the person who truly knows God that captivates us and inspires us to new levels of truth.

The obedience of Moses, the boldness of Elijah, the heartbeat of David, and the faith of Abraham came as a result of their intimate relationship and knowledge of God.

Without question you must purpose in your heart to know God, not with a "puppy-love" mentality that looks merely for benefits, but with a knowledge of God that brings Him into the supreme and rightful place of Lord over your life. Both God and mankind long for an intimate relationship together. God reaches out, and we must reach up.

Discovering the majesty of God becomes the inspiration that motivates you to seek to know Him more intimately.

The prophet Hosea spoke out to Israel and said, "Hear the word of the LORD, you children of Israel, for the LORD *brings* a charge against the inhabitants of the land: 'There is no truth or mercy or knowledge of God in the land'" (Hosea 4:1).

God clearly states the cause of His covenant people's falling away. They had allowed the important issues of life to go by the wayside. But God wanted them restored. He was reaching out to them as He reaches out to you. His objective is to create a sense of confidence and joyful stability in your relationship.

We need to be aware of what brings growth to a person's life. One of the most damaging wedges between two people is a sense of insecurity because of a lack of commitment toward each other. God wants you to be aware of His continued commitment to your life.

He longs for the commitment of your heart to know Him with an ever increasing depth. Three areas promote growth: truth, mercy, and the knowledge of God. Where these are lacking there exists a cold or lukewarm religious form.

Notice what happens with a lack the knowledge of God: "My people are destroyed for lack of knowledge…" (v. 6). The same point is emphasized again in Isaiah 5:13: "Therefore my people have gone into captivity, because they have no knowledge…."

People are destroyed and taken captive because of a failure to deeply know God and what He responds to. The people of Israel had turned away from their knowledge of God and they were reaping calamities—a harvest of their disobedience. Many Christians today have failed to understand that their own problems are largely the consequences of the same cause—lack of a true knowledge of God.

It is not the desire of God for His people to live under the fear and pressure of financial and economic crisis. The fear of what the future holds has turned many from experiencing joy to fatalistic depression. The fear of failing health, the dread of divorce, or the mental torment of dreams crumbling can be an emotional prison.

When people quit compromising their own desires and begin to set aside the time and effort to know Who God is, they will be lifted out of hopelessness into the life of abundance that Jesus came to provide.

God has given specific instructions in order to prevent His people from remaining in bondage:

Now acquaint yourself with Him, and be at peace; thereby good will come to you. Receive, please, instruction from His mouth, and lay up His words in your heart.

If you return to the Almighty, you will be built up; you will remove iniquity far from your tents. Then you will lay your gold in the dust, and the gold of Ophir among the stones of the brooks. Yes, the Almighty will be your gold and your precious silver; for then you will have your delight in the Almighty, and lift up your face to God.

You will make your prayer to

Him, He will hear you, and you will pay your vows. You will also declare a thing, and it will be established for you; so light will shine on your ways (Job 22:21-28 NKJV).

He said, "...acquaint yourself with Him." That is the key to peace in your mind. Becoming familiar with Him is the way in which great gain will come to you in every area of your life.

He is the most precious part of life—a treasure beyond value. When we look to the Lord, we have an assurance that He is ever present and willing to reveal His goodness to us and surround us with His favor.

Faith in God becomes as common as your breath. The Bible teaches in Romans 10:17, "So then faith comes by hearing, and hearing by the word of God." Why does the Word of God create faith? It is because every word in the Bible brings a revelation of Who

God is: His nature, His power, His desires. The words are energized with spiritual power that shows God to the reader or the listener.

The deeper you know God, the stronger your faith. The struggle for faith is replaced by the realization that God is faithful and trustworthy; then your faith develops without a struggle.

Hosea 6:3 says, "Let us know, let us pursue the knowledge of the LORD. His going forth is established as the morning...."

I don't know anyone who loses sleep wondering whether or not the sun will rise in the morning. When you "press in" to truly know God's character, you discover that He can be relied on and trusted. He is far more faithful and unchangeable than the rising of the sun each morning.

Developing Relationships

I have friends whom I have come to

know well. I like them, but I know that if I ever wanted them to be at my house at 7 p.m., they would be late. My lack of faith in their being on time is based on my knowledge of them. They don't know what it means to be on time.

When you know someone it becomes easy to have faith in them. You know what they will do. For instance, over the years, my wife, Vikki, and I have come to know each other's likes and dislikes. I know what food she likes. Many times I know just what she will order in a restaurant before she looks at the menu. We've come to the place that, in many ways, we think alike and enjoy the same things. We have come to know one another well.

As a strong relationship develops, you will find that your likes and dislikes become more like God's. You enjoy His presence. The more you pursue knowing the depth of His character and learn His ways, the more you think as He thinks and feel as He feels.

It is only natural when two people spend time together that the person with the weaker personality begins to take on the character of the stronger. You are influenced by those with whom you associate.

The Holy Spirit wants to over-shadow and change your carnal mind so that He can communicate His words, thoughts, and attitudes to your inner being; thus bringing your mind and emotions into perfect harmony with His will. This will take a diligent commitment to the Word of God on your part, as well as a sensitivity to His promptings.

The way you really get to know anyone is by spending time with them. When I first saw Vikki, I immediately began to devise a plan to meet her. Once we met, I developed a plan to continue seeing her. And through the years we've become a truly great team.

Many people want a powerful relationship with God, but they will not discipline themselves to seek God in order to obtain it. So they feel defeated before they ever begin. They cannot see themselves really living close to Him. As long as that kind of thinking dominates them, they are destined to a shallow Christian experience. But when they begin to chart the course of their lives and put God first, they will find Him quickly showing Himself strong to them.

Proverbs 3:6 from *The Amplified Bible* says: "In all your ways know, recognize, and acknowledge Him, and He will direct and make straight and plain your paths."

As you seek to know the Lord, you will find the direction you need. *The Living Bible* paraphrases it this way: "In everything you do, put God first, and he will direct you and crown your efforts with success." God crowns you with abundant living when you seek Him first.

There is a vast difference between knowing a person's actions and knowing what is deep in his heart. It is the same with God. When I speak of knowing God, I am not merely referring to His actions, but much more. Knowing God means knowing His character and qualities; then, going beyond the recognition of what they are and experiencing those qualities. The final results will be the reflection of them in your life.

Psalm 103:7 says, "He revealed his will and nature to Moses and the people of Israel." Israel saw the mighty acts and miracles God performed. They witnessed the plagues upon Egypt, the dividing of the Red Sea, water gushing from a rock, and the manna sent from heaven to feed them. Israel saw miracle after miracle, but despite what they saw, they continued to accuse God and curse His servants.

Moses, however, saw the same miracles but understood far more. He knew God! Deep within, he knew a God of righteousness and justice.

What made Moses different? There was a uniqueness about Moses that separated him from the other men of his day. His prayer in Exodus 33:13 gives us a glimpse of the desires that were important to him.

> *Now therefore, I pray You, if I have found favor in Your sight, show me now Your way, that I may know You [progressively become more deeply and intimately acquainted with You, perceiving and recognizing and understanding more strongly and clearly] and that I may find favor in Your sight* (AMP).

His heart was so tuned to God that

knowing His outward actions was not enough. Moses sought such a closeness between himself and God that he could clearly understand the desires of God's heart and know what brought joy to Him.

God is looking for people whose hearts are devoted to Him because of Who He is, and not for what He does. These are the people to whom He will show Himself strong. The people who want to bring delight and pleasure to the heart of their Heavenly Father, who will seek Him diligently, and will come to understand His ways.

Proverbs 2:1-5 gives sound guidance to bring you into an intimate fellowship with God.

My son, if you will receive my sayings, and treasure my commandments within you, make your ear attentive to wisdom, incline your heart to understanding; for if you cry for discernment, lift your voice for understanding; if you seek her as silver, and search for her as for hidden treasures; then you will discern the fear of the LORD, and discover the knowledge of God (NAS).

God gives clear direction to act upon. Seek Him and search for His wisdom as you would for treasure, then you will discover new depths of the knowledge of God.

The Apostle Paul was of the same breed as Moses. He had a longing to become intimate with God in order to be effectively used by Him. In Philippians 3:10, there is a prayer very similar to what Moses had prayed hundreds of years before. Again from *The Amplified Bible,*

For my determined purpose is that I may know Him [that I may progressively become more deeply and intimately ac-

quainted with Him, perceiving and recognizing and understanding the wonders of His Person more strongly and more clearly].

At the time Paul prayed this, he was not a novice in the ways of God. He had spent years after his conversion preparing for ministry. He had been on many journeys and seen every type of miracle and manifestation of God imaginable. He had seen visions and even been taken up into heaven to behold things he was not allowed to speak of on earth. Yet after all these great things, his prayer and the yearning of his heart was that he might know Him.

Paul remained humbly teachable by the Holy Spirit in order that he might understand the wonders of His Person. What a giant in the Kingdom of God! Paul never lost sight of the fact that to truly make God known to the world *you* must know Him and His innermost nature. Paul cried out to know the resurrection power of God exerted in and through him.

Many would try to discourage us with the idea that we can never really know God because we are not on His level. But the very fact that we are made in His image and likeness means we have the capacity not only to know Him, but to reveal Him.

The message of the Gospel is that Jesus Christ came down to the level of sinful man to lift us to the level of a Holy God. Our hope rests in what Jesus has accomplished in bringing us to the level of fellowship with God that He desires in the beginning. Jeremiah 9:23 (NAS) says:

> *Thus says the LORD, 'Let not a wise man boast of his wisdom, and let not the mighty man boast of his might, let not a rich man boast of his riches;*

*but let him who boasts boast of
this, that he understands and
knows Me, that I am the LORD
who exercises lovingkindness,
justice, and righteousness on
earth; for I delight in these
things,' declares the LORD.*

Throughout God's Word, He clearly
reveals that He will give us His wisdom, His might, and His riches, but
they are not the areas for boasting. Instead, they are the tools we use to accomplish the things in which He de-
lights: lovingkindness, justice, and
righteousness.

We want the wisdom, might, and
riches to make God known in the
earth, but our boasting must remain
in the fact that we can truly know and
understand Him.

In Daniel 11:32 it says, "...but the
people who know their God shall be
strong, and carry out great exploits."
When we know the Lord, we can effec-

23

tively make Him known. It's my desire to do the exploits of God; reaching up for His strength, and reaching out to make Him known.

Know Him, then make Him known. We are only left on the earth to live among men for a season. Let us faithfully represent Him while we are here.

CHAPTER 2

Alone With God

You can never come to know God deeply with shallow conversation. Intimacy with Him requires development and cultivation. The deepest working of the Holy Spirit comes during the time spent alone in His presence.

When we set time aside for fellowship with God we are entering into the richest experience of the Christian life. You were created for fellowship with Him. This alone satisfies the desire of mankind and of God. The fellowship and deep working of the Spirit is richest when you are set apart from things that clutter your mind.

Jesus said in Matthew 6:6, "But you, when you pray, go into your room, and when you have shut your door, pray to your Father who *is* in the secret *place;* and your Father who sees in secret will reward you openly."

It may sometimes feel as though you must drag yourself into the presence of God. Even when you are physically alone, your mind can be racing in many directions. You can easily waste that precious time with God by letting your mind wander. But Jesus said to enter the chamber and shut the door. Close the door of your mind on distractions that draw your attention away from Him and bring your mind under control.

Worship is one of the most powerful ways to bring your entire being into an attitude of receptiveness to God. As you enter into a time of fellowship with God, begin by worshiping Him. Sing a worshipful song, speak your adoration out loud to Him. Soon you will find that all of those things clamoring in your mind will take their rightful place—outside the door of your *inner chamber.* This is not time for your requests, but rather to simply enter His presence, enjoy His fellowship, listen for His promptings, and obtain the childlike assurance that your Father is near.

It is in these times of closeness to God that you have the greatest understanding of His willingness to be involved in your life. Your confidence will gain new strength, your emotions will be established, and your appreciation for all that He is will deepen. You can trust Him as never before because you know Him as never before.

In Jeremiah 17:7-8, there is a beautiful description of one who has learned to trust God: "But happy is he who relies on the Eternal, with the Eternal for his confidence! He is like a tree planted beside a stream, reaching its roots to the water; untouched by any fear of scorching heat, its leaves are ever green, it goes on bearing fruit in days of drought, and lives serene" *(Moffatt).*

Your time in the inner chamber causes your roots to reach deep into God. Deep roots make strong, healthy trees. In fact, most trees have as much under the ground in a root system as they do above the ground in branches and leaves. The root represents your private life with God. The leaves are the public life that others see. When a life of private fellowship is developed it will be evident as you minister and deal with people publicly.

For many, the vast majority of their time with God is in a public setting—either church, Bible study, or prayer meetings. You need as much substance beneath the surface of your life as you have above the surface.

Deep roots create stability and confidence in times when winds buffet you. There is tranquility and serenity deep within because you have tapped into the source of strength. When everything in your Christian experience is above the ground, you have very little depth of stability. No wonder you lack confidence in God. You can be so easily tossed back and forth.

It is in the quiet times in the presence of the Lord worshiping, waiting, praising, and listening that you enter the highest levels of prayer. You have left business outside the door and simply opened yourself to commune with your Father. These are the times God will speak to you and show you His wisdom and His will. Notice Psalm 81:13-16, again from the *Moffatt* translation:

> *Oh that my people would listen to me, that Israel would live my life! I would soon subdue*

*their foes, and strike at their op-
pressors; those who hate them
would cower before them, in unending terror; and I would feed
them with the finest wheat, with
honey from the rock to their
heart's content.*

The Results of Listening

God is clearly stating what His
people will experience if they will listen! Their enemy would be subdued,
and God would supply them with the
finest in life. The Lord offers His wisdom and direction to any who will
reach out and obtain it. It comes to
those who listen and live as God leads.

You find many references in the
life of Jesus where time alone to hear
from His Heavenly Father was vital. In
fact, His life was characterized by continually looking to His Father for guidance, direction, and fellowship. The
night before He chose His 12 disciples,

He went alone to the mountains to pray. He said, "...the Son can do nothing of Himself, but what He sees the Father do; for whatever He does, the Son also does in like manner" (John 5:19). Jesus would see what the Father did as He separated Himself to be alone in prayer.

Communion with God sharpens your sensitivity to Him and to other people. A man who deeply understood this was G. C. Bevington.[1] He was an itinerant preacher who lived around the turn of the century. On one occasion he went to the woods to get the mind of God. He felt impressed to go to a certain town and conduct evangelistic meetings, but he wanted to be sure he was being led by the Lord.

He said, "I continued to wait long before God, so as to be definite and sure. I spent 48 hours longer in this

---

[1] Bevington, G. C., *Remarkable Miracles,* 1973, Logos International, Plainfield, New Jersey.

commodious hotel — the hollow log — making 120 hours, getting things straight from headquarters. I tell you it pays to know what we are doing when it comes to dealing with God. This is where the trouble is with so many; they jump to conclusions when they should go slow."

He spent five days in a hollow log alone in the presence of God to obtain complete confidence that he was hearing from Heaven.

Another time he spent nine days under an oak tree in prayer. Of that instance he said, "You may ask, 'Why did it take nine days to get an answer?' Simply because I could not get still enough any sooner."

Why do some people have such great experiences with God? Much can be traced back to the hours of prayer and communion with Him.

This does not mean that the effecttiveness of prayer can be measured by the clock. But we must see the link between a deep knowledge of God and the times alone with Him being influenced by His presence.

The important secret of knowing God and having His influence is time spent alone with Him, absorbing His power and being changed by His presence. Hasty visits to the inner chamber are deceptive. When our life is inconsistent it's because we pray hastily. Our prayers lack power because we have not entered the realm of faith that fellowship alone will produce.

In the classic book *Power Through Prayer*,[2] E. M. Bounds makes this statement: "Much time spent with God is the secret of all successful praying. Prayer which is felt as a mighty force is the mediate or immediate product of much time spent with God. Our short

---

[2] Bounds, E. M., *Power Through Prayer*, 1974, Zondervan Publishing House, Grand Rapids, Michigan.

prayers owe their point and efficiency to the long ones that have preceded them. The short prevailing prayers cannot be prayed by one who has not prevailed with God in a mightier struggle of long continuance."

It is the deep roots produced in *private* fellowship that bring power for *public* benefit. Jesus was led by the Holy Spirit into the wilderness. When He returned, He came in the power of the Spirit. He was led into a time of fasting and prayer before beginning His public ministry.

Jesus was not brought to this secluded spot so the devil could take shots at Him. He was there to complete His preparation for revealing the presence and power of His Heavenly Father. It was right at the end of this time that Satan tested Jesus in an effort to get Him to compromise and not fulfill God's plan. In the power of the Holy Spirit, Jesus took the Scriptures and beat everything Satan threw at Him. Then He returned to Galilee, and the Bible says the fame of Him spread through the whole region (Luke 4:14).

If only each young believer could learn from the beginning of his Christian walk the importance of this truth: *If Jesus Himself needed to go into the presence of His Father to be renewed and find guidance, how much more does today's child of God need to do this?*

An Outward Expression of an Inward Process

In Exodus 34, Moses fasted in the presence of the Lord for 40 days and nights when he was given the Ten Commandments. Now notice verse 29: "Now it was so, when Moses came down from Mount Sinai...that Moses did not know that the skin of his face shone while he talked with Him."

When Moses stood in the presence

of God, there was a very dramatic outward effect—an unconscious effect. Moses was not even aware of the shine of God's glory on his face. Through communion in the inner chamber, your life and attitudes will be affected in such a way that will result in an outward expression of inward progress. You may not shine as Moses did but the evidence of your time with Him will be no less impressive.

As you enter into God's presence in worship and shut out the distractions of your mind, you step into the Holy of Holies. It is the sanctuary of the Lord, and you enter in spirit to the place of nearness to God. In Ezekiel 44:15-16 we find priests who were faithful to minister unto God in the sanctuary.

> *"But the priests, the Levites, the sons of Zadok, who kept charge of My sanctuary when the children of Israel went*

*astray from Me, they shall come near Me to minister to Me; and they shall stand before Me to offer to Me the fat and the blood," says the Lord G*OD*. "They shall enter My sanctuary, and they shall come near My table to minister to Me, and they shall keep My charge."*

Those who keep ministry to the Lord first place in their lives will enter into deep and intimate service to the Lord.

These sons of Zadok continued to enter the sanctuary even when others had abandoned God. They were told not to wear anything into the inner court that caused them to perspire. Then, when they went to the outer court to minister to the people, the clothes they wore while ministering to Him in the sacred chambers were left behind so they would not become contaminated.

Jesus Has Prepared the Way

When you come into His presence you know that Jesus has already gone before you to prepare the way. You can enter with complete confidence that you belong, because He has given you His robe of righteousness through your simple faith in Him. It is not by your own perspiration, not even your work for God, that brings you near to Him, but only by your confidence in Jesus' sacrifice and a willingness to enter.

He said, "They shall come near to me to minister to me." This is service to God that can be done no other way. You must come before Him. You cannot serve Him from a distance. The outer court is where you approach people, but the inner court is where you approach God.

Many times we feel that all we do in the outer court gives us a good excuse for not drawing near to God in the inner court. But without closeness to God through fellowship and ministry to Him in your inner chamber, you will find that your busyness with people—even ministry to them—is being done more to gratify your flesh than to build the Kingdom of God.

It seems, for the most part, that there is a lot of sweat in today's ministries and little waiting quietly in the presence of God to obtain His counsel and wisdom. I want God to look at me and my service to Him and say as He did about the sons of Zadok, "He shall be my minister and shall stand before me."

Input Determines Output

Your input will determine your output. If you will simply allow God to open your life and draw you close to Him, His very presence will saturate you with His influence. He will put *in* you the things that He wants to flow *through* you. It becomes a beautiful relationship that continues to increase as you become more and more comfortable being alone with Him.

CHAPTER 3

Seeking God's Ways

*Sow for yourselves righteous-
ness, reap in mercy; break up
your fallow ground, for it is time
to seek the LORD, till He comes
and rains righteousness on you*
(Hosea 10:12).

There are two kinds of Christian
hearts: the fallow heart and the
plowed heart. Fallow ground is uncul-
tivated, unused, idle, and dormant. It
was probably plowed at one time, but
because it remained untended, it
hardened and became crusted until
finally it needed to be broken up again
in order to become useful.

In the same way, the heart of a fallow-life Christian is content with himself; content with whatever fruit he may have produced in the past. He is tolerant of the self-searching of those earnestly seeking God. Yet he remains undisturbed. He has lost his passion for the presence of God in his life. He looks back with satisfaction at the glory that once was. He has lost the spirit of adventure.

The plowed life is the life that has remained prepared for the fresh activity of the Spirit. Discontented with the inactivity of the fallow field, he yearns to be cultivated and developed to receive seed again and again. He sees that his purpose is to be the habitation of seed.

Without the proper environment, seed cannot grow. The miracle of growth can only happen in cultivated ground. God's Words are God in seed form. All of God's Words contain the power necessary to cause them to bear fruit in your life. When you plant seed for a flower, all of the color of the bloom, the size of its petal, and every aspect of that type of flower will be contained in the seed.

God wants His seed (His Word) planted in your life. That way, you can become all that God is. Then, His seed growing up within you begins to change you into His image.

Only the life that is plowed and cultivated is eligible to see the miraculous growth of God's seed. Miracles follow the plow. It is those who reach out in their spirit to seek and know God's ways that become usable soil.

Diligently seeking the Lord is the open door to breaking up the hardened, unusable ground in your life. Notice the *Moffatt* translation of this same verse, "...break up your fallow ground, by seeking knowledge of the Eternal...."

There is a depth of spiritual power that God desires for you. You are the only one who can determine how much of that depth will be attained. "As the deer pants for the water brooks, so pants my soul for You, O God. My soul thirsts for God, for the living God...deep calls unto deep..." (Psalm 42:1-2, 7).

The deep longing and yearning of your inner man is to know God and His ways more intimately. That is God's desire for you. Psalm 63:1-2 from *The Amplified Bible* says,

> *O God, You are my God, earnestly will I seek You; my inner self thirsts for You, my flesh longs and is faint for You, in a dry and weary land where no water is. So I have looked upon You in the sanctuary to see Your power and Your glory.*

How far are you willing to go to quench the thirst that is within you?

Some people are just not determined enough, or desperate enough to seek the Lord. Those who are willing to seek Him until He comes and rains righteousness upon them will experience the outpouring of the Spirit in a new dimension.

The more deeply you yearn for God to pour Himself through you, the more deeply He will cultivate you. *Fruitfulness is always preceded by cultivation.* Seek Him until you experience the rain.

A Perfect Heart

For the eyes of the LORD run to and fro throughout the whole earth, to show Himself strong on behalf of those whose heart is loyal to Him (2 Chronicles 16:9).

A "heart perfect toward God" is a person who has devoted himself without reservation to God's ways; one who has the integrity to forsake his own ways when they conflict with God's; one who is pure in motive, dedication and sincere. God is always ready to supply power and sufficient strength to anyone who will open his heart with unqualified devotion to Him.

When the Holy Spirit is allowed only limited influence in your life, He is limited also in the results He can bring to you. It's not unusual to hear someone say they have tried to sow the seed of God's Word into their life, yet have seen very little fruit.

Notice what the Prophet Haggai said about people who see little fruit in their lives: "You have sown much, and bring in little; you eat, but do not have enough; you drink, but you are not filled with drink; you clothe your-selves, but no one is warm; and he who earns wages, earns wages to put into a bag with holes. Thus says the

LORD of hosts: 'Consider your ways!'"
(Haggai 1:6-7).

When your ways are not corre-
sponding to God's ways you will not
experience His power. But the Holy
Spirit will help you take hold of the
principles that produce increase. God
wants to reveal His ways to you. He is
reaching out to guide your ways and
to bring stability into your life. Some
people want His presence and power,
but not His demand for increasing ex-
cellence. It is the "half-dead" desire for
God's activity that has increased the
Church's ineffectiveness.

Carnal compromises have corrupted God's ways on the earth. Do
you really want God's presence to rule
in your life, or have you replaced the
challenges of God-inspired progress
with the false security of inaction?

In Genesis 6:12 we find it says,
"So God looked upon the earth, and
indeed it was corrupt; for all flesh had

corrupted their way on the earth." On a personal level, yielding to the flesh corrupts God's ways in your life. Our fellowship with the world has caused us to tolerate the flesh dominating our lives.

The world feeds the flesh with immorality, intellectualism, homosexuality, dishonesty, and adultery. Your flesh will follow after what it is surrounded with most frequently. But through fellowship with the Holy Spirit, you can discover how to yield to your inner man. You can begin to see more clearly the course God is taking and the mode of action He follows.

God's ways are filled with compassion, peace, righteousness, and power. Jesus was a revelation of the Father God. He was tender, yet He was unbending. He was filled with compassion, yet intolerant of sin. He ate with the outcasts and was ruthless toward religious snobs.

Our fellowship with Him affects our perception of things. We can begin to view things from God's viewpoint. When we start to surround ourselves with His influence, our fleshly desires start to lose their grip.

The only answer for the one who lives in a continual battle with his flesh and feels destined to non-productivity is this: Take a long, sober look at what is controlling your life. Then submit it to God and lay it aside. Let the Holy Spirit rise up in you and help you. He is ready and willing to support you on your journey to over-coming the compromise in your life. But He cannot do your standing for you.

There are some things that only God can do. And there are other things that only you can do. To expect God to do your part is to leave them undone. When you finally turn against weakness and compromise and put an end to justifying and protecting those things in your life, the Holy Spirit will become your strong support. That is the message of Romans 8:26.

Put an End to Evil Habits

In Romans 6:7, Paul clearly sets this goal for Christians: Sin and the flesh are not to rule over us. Then, in chapter 8, he describes how to attain that goal. "Therefore, brethren, we are debtors—not to the flesh, to live according to the flesh. For if you live according to the flesh you will die; but if by the Spirit you put to death the deeds of the body, you will live" (Romans 8:12-13).

The Twentieth Century New Testament states it this way: "...put an end to the evil habits of the body." Your flesh operates according to years of habits. But fellowship with God will begin to develop new habits in your life. Now look at Romans 8:26,

"Likewise the Spirit also helpeth our infirmities..." (*KJV*).

You can see from the context of this verse that the infirmities mentioned here have often been misunderstood. "Infirmities" mean our weaknesses and our inabilities to produce results. The Holy Spirit is prepared to help us in overcoming the areas of weakness we have tolerated. To understand how He does it, we must examine the word "helpeth." It means *to take hold together with someone against something.* The Spirit of God takes hold together with you against the weakness in your life. But *you* must be against that area of weakness. He cannot do it for you.

When I hear someone say they don't have the strength to overcome a weakness, they have said one of two things. "I don't know God well enough to know if He would help me," or "I am not yet willing to turn my back on that area of compromise and take hold of God's strength." God will take hold with you, but you must initiate it.

In Galatians 5:22-25, we have a description of what will flow in a person who is walking in the Spirit: "But the fruit of the Spirit is love, joy, peace, longsuffering, kindness, goodness, faithfulness, gentleness, self-control. Against such there is no law. And those who are Christ's have crucified the flesh with its passions and desires. If we live in the Spirit, let us also walk in the Spirit."

This fruit is a revelation of the nature of God. He *is* all of these. He has deposited His nature in us through the new birth. Through our fellowship with Him, our inner man (the spirit) gains ascendancy in our lives. We begin to take on the nature of our Father. The spirit begins to take control. This fruit is only indirectly the fruit of the Holy Spirit. When we model our lives after Jesus, this fruit begins to flow out of our human spirit.

When we pray in the Spirit we energize our inner man. As we act on the Word of God, His nature is built into us. This creates a new habit that does not respond to the impulses of the flesh, but instead draws from the resources of the Spirit.

This process is planting seed into your freshly cultivated spiritual field. In Galatians 6:8 the Lord promises: "You will reap a harvest. For he who sows to his own flesh (lower nature, sensuality) will from the flesh reap decay and ruin and destruction, but he who sows to the Spirit will from the Spirit reap eternal life" *(AMP)*. Your thoughts and inner life are where the seed-planting process begins. The decision as to the type of seed you sow is made in your mind. But only seeking carnal things will produce failures in the spiritual realm.

Developing the habit of sowing the seed of God's Word in your heart empowers your spiritual life. As you seek Him, you will begin to recognize His presence in your life in a much greater degree. You need not ask for God's presence; His presence and power are reality. But acknowledging Him when He manifests His presence and power will release God to accomplish His will in your life.

The Holy Spirit wants full possession of your heart. His desire is that the glory which He revealed in Jesus also be revealed in you. Jesus dwelt in flesh and blood to accomplish the work of the Holy Spirit. And the Holy Spirit also must dwell in flesh and blood to continue to accomplish His work on earth. You are that flesh and blood in which He dwells.

Let His creative power loose within you. It will cause inspired ideas to spring out of your spirit. Loose His wisdom and understanding. Release His ability. There is no shortage of God's ability and power, only a shortage of those willing to discover God's ways to release that ability and power.

Now notice Psalm 67:1-2, "God be merciful to us and bless us, and cause His face to shine upon us, Selah. That Your way may be known on earth, Your salvation among all nations."

The way to make God known is to first know His ways personally. As you observe His ways, you begin to change.

You take on the ways of the one you observe the most.

That is why it is so important to discover the ways of Jesus. It is also vital that you surround yourself with those who know Him.

The deeper you know Him, the more fully you can reveal Him. Just as the smell of cigarettes clings to your clothing when you walk through a smoke-filled room, in the same way, you take on a fragrance when you are in the presence of God. It is the aroma of the goodness of God on your life that draws people toward Him.

Let the Holy Spirit search deep within you. Open those previously reserved areas to Him and let His plow break up that hard, crusted ground. He will plant the most beautiful garden in what was once only wasteland.

Every selfish motive and thought will come under scrutiny of the Holy Spirit because He wants to transport you beyond the veil into the holiest place where the Father, the Savior, and the Holy Spirit live.

CHAPTER 4

Called Into Fellowship

As you look to the original idea God had for man, you see a beautiful picture of harmony and tranquility; people in fellowship with God. And because even their thoughts were toward God, their every need and desire was supplied.

God's original plan for man was the Garden of Eden where every need was supplied. And His plan to meet our every need has never changed. What a marvelous plan. The first chapters of Genesis reveal that God wanted mankind to live in a glorious relationship with Him to the extent that man would have no real concern about his needs, because they were all supplied.

The heart of God longed for companionship. When He made man, He made him in His own image and likeness because He wanted someone on His own level with whom to commune. Although angels and other beings existed, they were not of the quality for true fellowship.

Children are born into a family because of the love and union of the parents. Most parents then desire to pour themselves into that child and create for him a life that is full and beautiful. Everything the parents have is used to accomplish that goal.

Likewise, our Heavenly Father desired His own offspring. He gave His children the right to receive all He had, and therefore, they can obtain the powerful and beautiful results that His fullness brings. Notice what John 1:16 says, "And of His fullness we have all received, and grace for grace."

God's desire and dream has always been to fellowship with someone on the same level of life. Man was in that position until he turned away from God and obeyed a rebel spirit—Satan. At that point, man's pure fellowship with God was destroyed. God began immediately to implement a plan to restore mankind to a fellowship that fulfilled His dream.

The redemption Jesus brought restored man to a position of intimate communion with God. Many people do not recognize just how far-reaching and complete this redemption is. But, through simple faith in the sacrifice of Jesus, man was put back into the kind of relationship with God that Adam had in the Garden.

If this is not true, then the work of Satan in the Garden would have been greater than the work Jesus accomplished on the cross. But we know that, through the death, burial, and resurrection of Jesus, the price for sin and separation from God was paid.

Now there is no need or reason for any person to be outside a deep, personal relationship with the Lord. The door has been thrown wide open. The invitation is to all. The purpose is the same as it was in the beginning—God's dream of companionship.

You are the object of that dream!

When Adam was hiding from the presence of God in the Garden, the sound of that beautiful, familiar voice rang out, "Adam where are you?" That same call toward God's children has remained alive throughout history. God is seeking a relationship with His people.

"God is faithful, by whom you were called into the fellowship of His Son, Jesus Christ our Lord" (1 Corinthians 1:9). You have actually been called by

God Himself into the same fellowship that God the Father has with Jesus. That calling is an invitation into a very personal and intimate relationship together. In fact, you have a divine summons into the same fellowship with the Father.

Many shrink away from the thought of a fellowship with God that is like that of Jesus and the Father. But it is our own lack of self-confidence that brings this negative reaction. We have been convinced through religious condemnation that God tolerates us, but has little pleasure in us. Consequently, guilt becomes the primary motivation for any action we take.

We pray only because we feel guilty if we don't. We go to church because we feel guilty if we miss. We give because we feel guilty for not having done more. With an understanding of this, many so-called religious leaders develop tremendous skill in creating guilt in people as a form of psychological manipulation.

God does not lead by guilt; instead, He leads by His Spirit. And He moves through those who pray according to His Word. He guides those who live according to His commandment of love. He directs us to be givers who are sensitive to His leadership in our giving.

God has sent His Spirit and His Word to lead us, not guilt and condemnation. The praying, the church attendance, and the giving must all be done, but we must approach each of these areas with the right motivation or they will be fruitless. They should grow out of a love toward God and toward the people He loves.

When we get a real understanding of how God sees us, the better understanding we'll have of the fellowship to which we have been summoned.

God's Treasures

Notice how Jesus reveals the Father's desire for His people in the following two parables:

Again, the kingdom of heaven is like treasure hidden in a field, which a man found and hid; and for joy over it he goes and sells all that he has and buys that field.

Again, the kingdom of heaven is like a merchant seeking beautiful pearls, who, when he had found one pearl of great price, went and sold all that he had and bought it (Matthew 13:44-46).

To understand these parables, you must know the central figure of the parable is God Himself. In this chapter of Matthew, Jesus related another parable in which a man sowed seed in a field, and an enemy came and sowed tares among the seeds. Jesus explained to His disciples that the man in this parable was the Son of Man, and the enemy was the devil.

Another parable in Luke, chapter 15, describes a father who had two sons. We call it the Parable of the Prodigal Son, but it is not a revelation of a son. Every verse reveals the father's attitude. The Heavenly Father is the main character in this parable as well. The two parables in Matthew 13:44-46 reveal something about the nature of God.

A man discovered a treasure buried in a field. The treasure was of more value to him than all that he owned. Being an honest man, he decided that if he could buy the field he would then own everything in the field. He hid the treasure again and sold all he owned to purchase the field, thereby obtaining the treasure.

Another man was looking for beautiful pearls and found one of the most superior quality he had ever seen. He said to himself, "That is the pearl I must have." He had to sell all that was of value to him to get the pearl.

The man spoken of in these two parables is God. But who is the treasure, and who is the pearl? *You* are the treasure. *You* are the pearl. When God sees you, He sees a treasure. And He was willing to go to any expense to have you as His own. It required the most expensive price that has ever been paid. But because God wanted *you,* Jesus came and paid that awesome price—His life for yours.

Jesus did not just pay this price for the mass of humanity. He paid this price for individual people like you. If you had been the only person to ever receive His sacrifice, He would have paid the same price just for you. Can you imagine that? You mean that much to Him. You are His most valuable treasure! He was willing to go to any length to make your fellowship with Him possible.

When you see the price that was paid from that perspective, you will begin to realize the value that God places on you. Value is determined by the price that is paid for something. Your value is revealed by the price God paid to make you His own—His only Son.

God's Extreme Love

What is it about you that would cause God to go to such extreme measures on your behalf? His plan for you from the beginning was to enjoy unending fellowship together. And He refuses to be denied the pleasure of seeing His plan come to pass. When He sees you, He sees all you can be in Jesus Christ. And when He sees the world, He sees all each person in it could be in Him.

When you realize this, you see as

God sees. It will lift you into intimate fellowship with Him. It will lift your personal dignity and self-esteem. You gain a new belief about *your* worth because you see yourself lifted by His love. Not only does it change your self-perception, but it also changes the way you see others. You begin to see the worth of people everywhere, because you see what they can become in Christ.

In Titus 2:14, Paul expresses it this way under the inspiration of the Holy Spirit: "Who gave himself for us, that he might redeem us from all iniquity, and purify unto himself a peculiar people, zealous for good works" (*KJV*).

This redemption brings purity with it. The terminology, "to purify for Himself a peculiar people" has been largely misunderstood, but when examined, it reinforces exactly what we have been looking at.

The word *peculiar* does not describe people who act ridiculous or strange but, rather, people who belong to God, who are His possession: "... then ye shall be a peculiar treasure unto me above all people" (Exodus 19:5 *KJV*). God was saying that His people, Israel, would be a treasure to Him above all other nations. This places us into the same pure fellowship that God intended when He placed man in the Garden.

Fellowship With God

The real tragedy is that today there are Christians who recognize their union *in* Christ, but have no communion *with* Christ. Through simple faith and acceptance of the sacrifice Jesus made for you, a union has taken place. You have been united with God. But the union alone is not the end of God's plan. Remember, He longed to fellowship with you. Fellowship becomes the communion. Our pursuit for fellowship with the Lord is what makes our union with Him vibrant and alive.

It is a sad reality that God is no more real to many Christians than He is to unbelievers. These Christians have accepted the union, but denied God their communion. Notice John 15:4 from the *Wuest* translation:

> *Maintain a living communion with me, and I with you. Just as the branch is unable to be bearing fruit from itself as a source unless it remains in a living union with the vine, so neither you, unless you maintain a living communion with me.*

Just as a branch draws its life-giving sap from the vine, so you and I draw the flow of God's life through our intimate times of communion in His Word and prayer. One reason people waver in their confidence with God is because they deny themselves the privilege of consistent communion and fellowship with their Heavenly Father.

Jesus goes on to say, "If you maintain a living communion with me and my words are at home in you, I command you to ask, at once, something for yourself, whatever your heart desires, and it will become yours. In this my Father is glorified, namely, that you are bearing much fruit. So shall you become my disciples" (vs. 7-8 *Wuest*).

God's Word becoming fruitful in and through you is directly linked to the maintaining of a living, rich, continuing fellowship with the Lord. The richness of God's life does not come from a one hour, Sunday-morning experience. That works no better than a marriage whose partners express their love at a predetermined time once each week.

Instead, it is the freedom to come to God spontaneously and pour your love out to Him, and receive love from Him, that creates a viable and powerful relationship. Look again at First Corinthians 1:9 from *The Amplified Bible.* "God is faithful—reliable, trustworthy and [therefore] ever true to His promise, and He can be depended on; by Him you were called into companionship and participation with His Son, Jesus Christ our Lord."

Call to Companionship

Called into companionship with the Lord means to *go* where He is going and to *do* what He is doing. You can be a companion of Jesus. You are no longer linked to the darkness in this world, but He has delivered you from darkness and shone His light within you. Light now shines in you —the light of the gospel—and that is where the power is.

A companion is one who walks side by side with another. Not tagging along far behind, but together—

united. We walk in light with Him. We were once in darkness, but He has brought us into His light. Ephesians 5:8-9 from the *Weymouth* translation says:

> *There was a time when you were nothing but darkness. Now, as Christians, you are Light itself. Live and act as sons of light —for the effect of the Light is seen in every kind of goodness, uprightness and truth.*

As a companion to the Author of Light, you reveal the effects of that light in your inner being. You demonstrate His goodness. You walk in uprightness. You manifest the truth. This is when your participation begins to come. As you demonstrate that His goodness is toward people everywhere, those around you see God in a new perspective. Romans 2:4 says that it is God's goodness, not tragedy, that leads men to repentance.

The Dual Effect of Light

God's light in you has a dual effect. First, it frees you from the effects that darkness and corruption had upon you. Second, it flows out of you in the form of goodness, uprightness, and truth. These are powerful forces that bring God's abilities to the forefront through you.

Notice First Peter 2:9 from the *Phillips* translation,

> *But you are God's 'chosen generation,' his 'royal priesthood,' his 'holy nation,' his 'peculiar people'—all the old titles of God's people now belong to you. It is for you now to demonstrate the goodness of him who has called you out of darkness into His amazing light.*

The Scripture reveals that God is reproducing Himself in you! Then He can demonstrate Himself to the world through you. Begin the adventure of unhindered fellowship with your Heavenly Father. Make communion with Him your number one priority.

CHAPTER 5

The Fatherhood of God

Jesus came as a revelation of the heart of God. His teachings, miracles, and healings all revealed an attitude about God that had not been understood before—God wanted to do special things in the lives of people.

As Jesus taught, the people were overwhelmed by His message. In Luke 4:22 it says, "So all bore witness to Him, and marveled at the gracious words which proceeded out of His mouth...." The way we might say that today is: "They wondered at His words of grace."

The reason the people were filled

with awe was because the tradition taught at that time by religious leaders was without grace. But Jesus went beyond the limits of what the people had ever heard.

He declared God as His Father. The very idea stirred indignation and wrath in the religious mind because they understood the implications of what Jesus was saying.

With these words Jesus put Himself on an equal level with God. The people cried out, "Blasphemy." This was an outrage. No one called God "Father." It was unheard of. But Jesus' message did not stop there. His message was to reveal that God's deep desire was to be *your* Father.

Throughout Matthew, chapters 5-7, Jesus referred to God as *your* Father which is in heaven. This was absolutely revolutionary. Jesus emphasized this idea in depth with the parable of the prodigal son.

The word "prodigal" has the connotation of rebellion and stubbornness; of a person running from God. But "prodigal" is not a biblical word. It is a word tradition has added to our biblical vocabulary. Tradition also has assigned it to the lost son in Luke 15:11-24.

The central figure of this parable is not the son, as we pointed out in chapter 4. From the beginning to the end, the father is the center of attention. It is the response of the father that brings real insight. This is a revelation of a prodigal father, not a prodigal son. This father reveals the Heavenly Father's attitude.

In order to truly understand the picture Jesus is portraying of the Father, you must first understand the true meaning of the word *prodigal*. Webster's *New Twentieth Century Dictionary* defines it as given to extravagant expenditures, lavish, extremely abundant.[1] If you think about it, that describes the father in this parable much more than the son. The father was extravagant with his love. He lavished his goodness upon his son even though the son squandered his goods. And he was abundantly confident that his son would return.

When the son left he took with him the portion of goods that belonged to him. Under the legal system of that time the eldest son received a double portion of the family inheritance. The younger son received a single portion which, in this case, would be one-third of the family's possessions.

The younger son took his inheritance and squandered it away. Finally, he found himself at the point of desperation and took a job feeding swine. For a Hebrew, feeding swine was a degrading position. Even among other na-

---

[1] Webster's *New Twentieth Century Dictionary,* 2nd ed., S.V. "prodigal."

tions it was a demeaning occupation.

Among the Egyptians, swine herders were completely cut off from society. But this man was a Hebrew, one of God's chosen people, a man with a covenant with God Almighty. And yet, he was at the bottom of society.

Why is it that we wait until everything looks hopeless before we look to our Heavenly Father for help? It seems that things must be desperately out of control before we reach out to God. That is not God's intention. He does not want you to experience even the slightest break in receiving His inheritance. When you remain in fellowship with God, you continue to receive from the abundant supply of His inheritance.

This son squandered his inheritance by going into a far country, away from the fellowship and guidance of his father. Many times Christians squander their inheritance also.

They let God's blood-bought provision slip through their fingers when they fail to realize that they are accepted by God. They do not understand their identity in Christ.

A New Creation

Even though they are a new creation, delivered from Satan's power, they live according to old habit patterns; dominated by the evil one. This is not necessarily outright rebellion, but rather, a failure to explore the potential that dwells within every true believer.

The prodigal father's response to his son's reappearance was not the way many parents might have responded. Some would have disowned their son for squandering the family inheritance. Others might have made him pay back every dollar he wasted. Still others might have threatened to shoot him if he dare put one foot on their property.

Many parents wonder what they should do when their wandering children return to them for help. They should do what this man did: Look with great anticipation for their children's return. This father saw his son afar off. Everyday he looked to the horizon expecting his son to come home. Then when he saw him, he ran to him and surrounded his son with compassion and love. That is what will win your children. Stand on the Word of God, expecting their return, and continuing in the fullness of God's love—no matter what they have done.

The moment you move toward living in the full potential of your inheritance, God will reach out to lift you into His best. God is always expectant. This prodigal father continued to lavish things on his son as we find in Luke 15:22-24.

> *But the father said to his servants, 'Bring out the best robe*

*and put it on him, and put a
ring on his hand and sandals
on his feet. And bring the fatted
calf here and kill it, and let us
eat and be merry; for this my
son was dead and is alive
again; he was lost and is
found.' And they began to be
merry.*

Notice the father did not pay any
attention to the son's carefully re-
hearsed speech of unworthiness. He
did not even allow him to finish what
he was saying. The father called to his
servants to bring three things to the
son. Each has significance in what
God has done for you.

The best robe. This was the robe
worn by the father himself. The father
took his own robe and put it on his
son. Isaiah 61:10 refers to this robe: "I
will greatly rejoice in the Lord, My soul
shall be joyful in my God; for He has
clothed me with the garment of salva-

tion, He has covered me with the robe of *righteousness*, as a bridegroom decks himself with ornaments, and as a bride adorns herself with her jewels."

When you recognize that God's own robe of righteousness has been placed on you, it is a cause for great joy. You are welcome in the very throne room of God. You belong there! This God of grace is your loving Father. He lifts you out of guilt into freedom.

Jesus identified with your sin through the cross so you could identify with His righteousness by faith in His redemption. Now you are clothed with His righteousness. You have been elevated into companionship with God the Father.

The ring. This was the ring of authority within the household. The ring restored dignity. He once again had the rights as a member of the family.

Notice what John 1:12-13 says about our rights are sons:

> *But as many as received Him, to them He gave the right to become children of God, to those who believe in His name: who were born, not of blood, nor of the will of the flesh, nor of the will of man, but of God.*

As a son, you have received rights in the Kingdom of God and authority on the earth through your sonship.

The shoes. When the son returned, he came as a barefooted slave. But the father removed that slave attitude and put shoes on his feet. He was not an outcast any longer, he was once again a son. He was not looked down on as a rebel, he was received and restored.

Now it was time to celebrate! The father had a calf already fattened and *they began to be merry.* When the son had gone into the far country, the Bible says, *he began to be in want.* When he returned home he could be merry.

The far country in this parable is the realm of rebellion. It is a condition of the soul, a way of thinking that cuts off fellowship with God. Setting aside God's desire and goals will bring you to the place of want. When you return to your Father you can receive:

The kiss of compassion.

The robe of righteousness.

The ring of authority.

The shoes of a son.

What an extravagant blessing this father gave his son!

In the book *The Life and Times of Jesus the Messiah,*[2] Alfred Edersheim states that there is an absolute contrast between this teaching of Christ and one of the oldest rabbinic works.

---

[2] Edersheim, Alfred, *The Life and Times of Jesus the Messiah,* 1972, William B. Eerdmans Publishing Company, Grand Rapids, Michigan.

This parable is exactly the opposite of the one in the Bible. In the rabbinic parable, the son of a friend is redeemed from bondage, not as a son, but to be a slave so that obedience might be demanded of him.

God is not looking for stone-cold obedience, but rather, a warm fellowship. Through fellowship with God a desire will rise up within you to do the things that are pleasing in His eyes.

The prodigal father saw something beyond his right to demand obedience. He recognized the great potential which remained in his son. He wanted his son's potential developed, and he wanted his son restored.

Whenever you turn to God, you'll find Him looking, longing, and waiting for your return. God is ready to restore you and lift you to your potential.

Acts 20:32 says, "So now, brethren, I commend you to God and to the word of His grace, which is able to build you up and give you an inheritance among all those who are sanctified."

It is the Word of His grace which will lift you. It will build your life and reveal your potential in Him. The grace of God which is freely given to you will bring you into new levels of your inheritance, for you *have* received an inheritance.

Two Inheritances

There are two types of inheritances. First is the inheritance you receive at the death of a loved one. If you were listed in their will you receive according to that will. You may inherit money, furniture, property, etc. These are the benefits of the inheritance. Psalm 103:2-5 describes our benefits:

Bless the Lord, O my soul, and forget not all His benefits; who forgives all your iniquities, who heals all your diseases, who redeems your life from destruction, who crowns you with lovingkindness and tender mercies, who satisfies your mouth with good things, so that your youth is renewed like the eagle's.

What great benefits! Jesus died and you received an inheritance. Then He rose from the dead to see to it that His will is carried out in your life.

There is a second type of inheritance. This is what you receive from your parents when you are born. You may inherit their eyes, ears, hair, nose, etc. The way you think and act is developed through your contact with them. You inherit their background and ancestry.

Now that you have been born into a new family you have a new background. Your ancestry is no longer just your earthly forefathers. Your ancestry is now God Himself. He is your background. You are born into His family. He is your inheritance and you have received His nature.

The more you are in contact with Him, the more your thinking and attitude is conformed to His. You have stepped into a new race of people. You are now a part of a holy nation—a new nation of people born of the blood of Jesus.

The more of a reality this becomes to you, the more you will live as a true heir of God. Whatever physical problems you might have inherited from your natural family no longer have authority in your body. You now possess the nature of this new family.

Divine health is passed on from your Heavenly Father. His nature of super-abundant supply can overcome any physical deformity or malfunction that may have been passed down through your natural family. God's power is more than enough, and that power is abiding within you.

Take hold of a new concept of your Heavenly Father. He has made His extravagance and abundance available to you. He is not holding back from you.

"Do not fear, little flock, for it is your Father's good pleasure to give you the kingdom" (Luke 12:32).

CHAPTER 6

The Shepherd of My Soul

The 23rd Psalm is considered by many to be the most beautiful passage in the entire Bible. It seems to articulate the desire of every heart: The need for guidance and care, the feeling of personal vulnerability, and yet the confidence that under the protective leadership of the Good Shepherd we will not be left to wander aimlessly in life.

The Lord God is the Shepherd of His people. We look to Him and He is the fulfillment of all our wants. He brings deep satisfaction to us, and we trust in His ability to shepherd us.

It is a great comfort to realize that God is watching out for you! You are part of His flock. If you will but follow His lead He will order your steps to find the right substance to sustain a strong spiritual relationship. If you will not wander from His lead you will be led to cool, clear waters that refresh and revive.

The psalmist David was clearly acquainted with the relationship between a shepherd and his sheep. His chore as a young man was to tend his father's flock. He knew, through experience, how helpless sheep become without a caring shepherd. Because of his intimate relationship with sheep, David could see the contentment in the flock as they trusted him.

David said, "The Lord is my shepherd..." (Psalm 23:1). With that statement he said something of God and of himself. Through the inspiration of the Holy Spirit, David revealed God as a good shepherd who leads His sheep to the green pastures and still waters of life. He saw God as a good shepherd who brought comfort and protection to His people. David saw himself as the recipient of all of the shepherd's goodness.

Jesus identified Himself as the Good Shepherd and at the same time affirmed His deity. He said, "I am the good shepherd..." (John 10:14). He made the intention of any good shepherd clear when He said, "...I have come that they may have life, and that they may have it more abundantly" (v. 10). He went on to say, "My sheep hear My voice, and I know them, and they follow Me" (v. 27).

Sheep that experience God's best are sheep that follow Him closely.

He will lift your soul from failure, depression, and lack into a wealthy place. He will restore your soul and life.

In looking at the soul, we find it very often misunderstood. The soul is not the spirit of man, though it is so closely linked that only the Word of God can bring a clear distinction. The soul is where we find the will, the emotions, the intellect, and the mind of man. It is in the soul that the seed of God's Word must be planted in order to bring about a change in lifestyle and experience.

The Seat of Power

The soul is the true seat of power. Without cooperation from the soul of a person, God's hands are almost completely tied in their life. However, with cooperation God's power will flow beautifully through any life.

When Jesus became Lord of your life, you became a new creation! You received a new source of your life— God Himself! He immediately began to initiate changes in your life. Changes that were not *imposed* from the outside; instead they were *inspired* from the inside. These changes began to restore your life.

Religion is often thought of in terms of rules that are imposed on people. Religious-minded people can size up anyone by simply comparing them with their imposed rules. But true change in a person comes from deep within. God begins to inspire them to change, and with the inspiration He empowers them.

It is from the soul that the choices of life are made. If you yield to the Holy Spirit, your choices will be influenced by His wisdom; and you will remain in the realm of His direct influence. But if you turn your thoughts and will away from God's perfect will you cut yourself off from the flow of His spiritual life and power.

Notice in Proverbs 23:7, "For as he thinks in his heart, so is he." The word for *heart* is from the word for soul. The way you think plants seeds into your life that will eventually grow into action. If you continually ponder and tolerate negative, destructive thoughts it will manifest through gossip and criticism. But if you flood your mind with godly, edifying, power-filled thoughts, it will manifest as you encourage and lift people with your words and actions.

When God created man, He breathed spiritual life into his soul. As long as man continued to walk with God, he experienced an uninterrupted flow of spiritual life and fellowship. But when man turned from following God and willfully followed another, he cut off his spiritual connection with God.

When Adam yielded to Satan's outward pressure he experienced an inward collapse—an *implosion*. The soul of man was lost. Satan approached Jesus in the same manner. Through outward pressure he hammered away at Jesus to bend His will to the point that He would not fulfill God's plan. When Jesus prayed in the garden He faced the challenge for all of mankind. He did not yield to the pressure, but through prayer and communion with His Father He drew the strength to say, "...not My will, but Yours, be done" (Luke 22:42).

Through his obedience He set the stage for the flow of God's life to once again dwell in man. Through His sacrifice He released an *explosion* from within the spirit of man that would release God's power through His soul and body.

To *restore* means "to bring back to a former or original condition; to put back in a former place of position—reinstate; to bring back to health or vigor; to give back something lost."[1]

---

[1] Webster's *New Twentieth Century Dictionary,* 2nd ed., S.V. "restore."

The psalmist said, "He restores my soul..." (Psalm 23:3). As you yield your mind, will, and emotions to the power of the Holy Spirit, God will restore to you what He originally planned for man.

Unlike your spiritual new birth, freedom coming to your soul comes step by step. As you begin to desire the things of the Spirit of God, your soul is renewed. It is expressed this way in James 1:21, "...receive with meekness the implanted word, which is able to save your souls." God's Word, which is born within you, has all that is necessary to bring freedom and liberty to your soul. As you continue to respond to God's Words, thoughts, and ways, you will be transformed to think like God.

In Psalm 19:7 we read, "The law of the Lord is perfect, converting the soul...." It is God's Word applied to your mind, will, and emotions that brings this conversion to your soul.

The word translated *converting* is the same word in Psalm 23:3 rendered *restore.* The Shepherd of your soul brings conversion and restoration into your life. It comes through His Word and your responsibility is to simply receive. You receive His thoughts! You receive His will! You receive His plans! And when you do they become yours and you become His expression.

Step by step you enter into the freedom to live as God created you to live. Satan is no longer stealing your success, for you do not respond to his influence nor act on his inspiration.

The Lord is your Shepherd. He directs, influences, and rules over your soul because you yield to His Word, His will, and His inspirations.

This idea of the Good Shepherd restoring your soul takes on a beautiful meaning when you know, as the shepherd David knew, the outcome of a stray sheep. Though it might be difficult to understand, even in the care of the finest shepherd, some sheep wander off from time to time. In the same way, even after we have walked with God for some time, we can feel as though we are flat on our back and need restoration.

Even David experienced defeat and the frustration of having walked into a snare. He could easily identify with the cry of another psalmist who said:

> *Why are you cast down, O my soul? And why are you disquieted within me? Hope in God...* (Psalm 42:11).

Only another shepherd as closely acquainted with sheep such as David could fully appreciate the significance of a *cast-down* sheep. This is a term used by old English shepherds for a sheep that has turned over on its back and is unable to get up again by itself.

Cast-Down Sheep

Phillip Keller was once a shepherd, and in his book entitled, *A Shepherd looks at Psalm 23,* he writes: "A 'cast' sheep is a very pathetic sight. Lying on its back, its feet in the air, it flails away frantically struggling to stand up, without success. Sometimes it will bleat a little for help, but generally it lies there lashing about in frightened frustration. If the owner does not arrive on the scene within a reasonably short time, the sheep will die."[2]

The way sheep become "cast" is very significant to us as Christians. Lying down to relax, the sheep rolls onto its side. But when the center of gravity in its body shifts, and its feet no longer touch the ground, it becomes completely helpless. When it cannot bring itself back to its feet, gases begin to build up in its stomach

---

[2] Keller, Phillip, *A Shepherd Looks at Psalm 23*, 1970, Zondervan Publishing House, Grand Rapids, Michigan.

which retard the blood circulation.

This alone could bring death to the sheep but there is another worry. The "cast" sheep has become an easy prey for any predator. It lies with its spindly legs straight up in the air, helplessly waiting to be found, hoping it will be found by its shepherd.

Look again at what causes the sheep to become "cast." The sheep found a comfortable place to lie down and relax. Proverbs 4:23 says, "Keep and guard your heart with all vigilance and above all that you guard, for out of it flows the springs of life" *(AMP)*. And Proverbs 19:15 says, "...an idle soul shall suffer hunger" *(KJV)*.

You will never find a safe place to relax your faith or set aside your self-discipline in God. Satan looks on with anticipation for that point of weakness when you lie down. You must continually guard your inner life to keep the springs of life flowing within you.

An alert shepherd knows each of his sheep and quickly recognizes when one is missing. When the sheep is found—realizing that each minute is critical—the shepherd tenderly rolls it over and stands it upright, rubbing its legs until the circulation returns. Guiding its steps, he leads it back into the secure surroundings of the flock.

The Shepherd's Heart

The shepherd's heart is revealed to us again in one of the parables of Jesus found in Luke 15:4-6:

What man of you, having a hundred sheep, if he loses one of them, does not leave the ninety-nine in the wilderness, and go after the one which is lost until he finds it?

And when he has found it, he lays it on his shoulders, rejoicing.

And when he comes home, he

calls together his friends and neighbors, saying to them, 'Rejoice with me, for I have found my sheep which was lost!'

This parable expresses God's attitude towards people who are "cast down" or lost. He rejoices when they are found. Jesus brought this revelation of the heart of His Father in direct response to the Scribes and Pharisees disapproval of the people Jesus associated with. This parable again contradicted the Pharisaical attitude which said, "There is joy before God when those who provoke Him perish from the world."

God reaches out to be a shepherd to the lost. But what does it mean to be lost? There is the lost feeling of having no personal relationship with God. It can mean the lost desire for guidance and direction from the shepherd and the "I'll-do-it-my-way" attitude. It can even be the lost sense of no longer feeling special to the important people in your life.

Indicators of a Lost Life

The greatest danger is when you do not know you have strayed but the indicators in your life show that you have: You have lost interest in people; you have become insensitive to the problems they bring upon themselves; you only have words filled with negativism, judgment, and criticism. You have actually lost contact with the true heart of God. You need a fresh experience with the Good Shepherd to be restored to real living.

When God finds men and women flat on their backs He reaches out to lift them, putting them back on their feet, getting the circulation flowing again, and brings them back to the protection of His rod and the direction of His staff.

He is the restorer of your soul. He

will fill you with new thoughts that will replace discouragement. He will bring clarity to His plans for you. He will free you from confusion and give you the comfort of knowing you belong.

Know that the Lord, He is God; it is He who has made us, and not we ourselves; we are His people and the sheep of His pasture (Psalm 100:3).

Know that He looks beyond your frailties and mistakes. His love is constant; it never changes. He does not get fed up with you; instead, He looks beyond today and sees the possibilities that lie ahead.

CHAPTER 7

Dynamic Living

The Holy Spirit expressed His desire for us through the prayer the Apostle Paul prayed for the Colossian church:

> *For this reason we also, since the day we heard it, do not cease to pray for you, and to ask that you may be filled with the knowledge of His will in all wisdom and spiritual understanding; that you may walk worthy of the Lord, fully pleasing Him, being fruitful in every good work and increasing in the knowledge of God; strengthened with all might, according to His glorious power,*

for all patience and longsuffering with joy; giving thanks to the Father who has qualified us to be partakers of the inheritance of the saints in the light. He has delivered us from the power of darkness and conveyed us into the kingdom of the Son of His love.... (Colossians 1:9-13).

The Lord's desire is that you increase in every area of your life. There is a simple progression that brings this increase. You may not grow to your full potential of fruitfulness overnight, but as a new lifestyle begins to emerge you will see the limitless possibilities ahead.

Notice first that His desire is that you be filled with a clear personal knowledge of His will for your life. Ephesians 5:17 in the *Phillips* translation says, "Don't be vague, but firmly grasp what you know to be the will of the Lord."

Yield to the Will of God

With each new discovery of God's will, make the determination to grasp onto it. Cling to it! Allow it to become firmly rooted within your heart. Begin to yield to His will.

With each new wave of understanding, yield yourself to His will in your life. It is God's will for you to be well. Yield to success. He is the God of the successful. Yield to the attitude of a giver. Yield yourself to increased prayer.

With every new revelation of God's will comes the demand for a new commitment. Rise up to receive all that He has for you.

It is only after you begin to see God's desire for you that you can go on to the next part of this progression.

"...That you may walk worthy of the Lord, fully pleasing Him..." (Colossians 1:10). When you realize that He has made you worthy, you can more easily walk in His will and become more pleasing to Him.

Understand that from the beginning you can by no means earn God's blessing in your life. His goodness is given by His grace and mercy. You *can,* however, limit God from working in you and through you. You prevent the goodness of God from getting to you through wrong thinking about God, or even a poor image of yourself.

To live "worthy" of the Lord means to conduct yourself in a suitable fashion, to act in a way which reflects God's character and thoughts. This worthiness actually means living as a display of the value and worthiness of Jesus.

Your manner of life expresses the value you place upon Jesus. Your life becomes a pleasure to God because you are conformed to His wishes, changed to His ways, and delighting in

His desires. Philippians 2:3-8 describes this manner of living:

Do nothing from selfishness or empty conceit, but with humility of mind let each of you regard one another as more important than himself; do not merely look out for your own personal interests, but also for the interests of others.

Have this attitude in yourselves which was also in Christ Jesus, who, although He existed in the form of God, did not regard equality with God a thing to be grasped, but emptied Himself, taking the form of a bond-servant, and being made in the likeness of men.

And being found in appearance as a man, He humbled Himself by becoming obedient to the point of death, even death on a cross (Philippians 2:3-8 *NAS*).

111

To esteem others as more important does not mean you put yourself down. It's God's desire to lift you up. You must see yourself from His vantage point. He has elevated you to the position of king and priest. You can now lift others.

When you have a strong self-esteem, you will not be threatened by others. When you discover that God's dream is to live in you and lift you onto His level of living, then you will discover that success is in Him—not in people.

You do not need to look out only for yourself. Because God is looking out for you, you can give attention to others, to their needs and hurts. You're not self-centered, you're God-centered; and you serve God as you serve other people. That is walking worthy of the Lord.

You know that "all things are yours." You are not just trying to get something, you are trying to give—giving of yourself, giving your prayer time, giving your money, giving to others from the power of God that is alive within you.

This is what makes life full and rich. Fulfillment comes from achievement, but lasting fulfillment comes from achievements in service to Christ and others.

Remember: To walk worthy of the Lord is to live in a manner that reflects God's character and thoughts. The attitude Jesus revealed was that of an obedient bond-servant, a slave of love, one totally given to the desires of His Father and to the deliverance of mankind.

Our Example

Jesus became the example of a New Testament man, a man born of the Holy Spirit with God as His Father. He emptied Himself of all divine rights and lived as a man subject to the direction of the Holy Spirit. Then, through His obedience, He brought freedom to mankind. Why are *you* to walk upright? So you can become fruitful. Your obedience to God brings freedom to people. Notice the results of obedience in Jesus:

> *Therefore also God highly exalted Him, and bestowed on Him the name which is above every name, that at the name of Jesus every knee should bow, of those who are in heaven, and on earth, and under the earth, and that every tongue should confess that Jesus Christ is Lord, to the glory of God the Father* (Philippians 2:9-11 *NAS*).

That is *increase*! It came because Jesus fulfilled the desire of His Father, He was a reflection of God's character, and His obedience brought deliverance to people everywhere He went.

There was no limit to His fruitfulness to God. He had consecrated His life fully. He pledged Himself before His Father, before the angels, and before mankind that He would not stop short of dying for the world.

Each day He subjected the desire of His mind and will to what He knew was the will of His Father. He demonstrated that a man relying on God as his source of strength can have victory over sin and Satan.

God's Divine Expression

What a great goal to reach for, and what a tremendous example Jesus gave us to imitate. When you see the impact of this new lifestyle, then you can understand why God sets such a high premium on His children living under the direction and guidance of the Holy Spirit. He is giving you the ability to be His divine expression so you more perfectly reflect His nature.

Certainly change is required to live

this dynamic life. But when you stepped out of the kingdom of darkness and into the fullness of the Kingdom of God, you immediately acquired the inherent ability to walk in God's light. You are now under the dominion of a new kingdom.

You possess a sufficient supply of His strength to successfully sever the undesirable attitudes that have restrained your progress. There is a deep need for positive change. The Apostle Peter describes some aspects of this needed change:

> *Therefore gird up the loins of your mind, be sober, and rest your hope fully upon the grace that is to be brought to you at the revelation of Jesus Christ; as obedient children, not conforming yourselves to the former lusts, as in your ignorance; but as He who called you is holy, you also be holy in all*

*your conduct, because it is writ-
ten, "Be holy, for I am holy"* (1
Peter 1:13-16).

Peter begins with an appeal to
bring your mind under control. The
mind is the real battleground. Old
habits and desires apply pressure to
your mind. Thoughts of negativism
and defeat try to dominate you.

Gird Up Your Mind

To "gird up the loins of your mind"
is to put out of your mind all the
things that will impede the progress of
God's power working through you —
such things as jealousy, fear, worry,
unforgiveness, and impurity. When
you harbor these things you prevent
the Holy Spirit from flooding your
mind with the creative, inspired ideas
that He tries to impart to you.

To be sober is to be calm and col-
lected in your spirit, to be temperate.
It brings your mind into a state of self-

control. You are able to see things clearly without distortion. Satan's attacks of worry and fear have an intoxicating effect when they are allowed to remain unchecked. They will produce a distorted or exaggerated view of situations which undermine the work of God's Word in your life.

Girding up the mind and soberness, together with an expectation of God's grace, create confidence that we can truly live holy and pleasing to God. Now our inward holiness begins to find outward expression. The word "holiness" seems to strike a note of condemnation in the minds of many. That generally stems from the way in which it is taught. To many, guilt and condemnation go hand-in-hand with holiness.

The rationale of some ministers is, "If I can make people feel real bad, then I have ministered on holiness." It seems that when they read the commission that Jesus gave Peter, they read it this way: "Peter, do you love me? Then *beat* my sheep." They have forgotten John 3:17 which says, "For God did not send His Son to condemn the world, but that the world through Him might be saved." That is just as important to the Gospel as John 3:16.

Understanding Holy Living

In order to truly understand the nature of God's demand for holy living you must perceive the purpose. God yearns to lift people everywhere into a successful and powerful experience in Him. He desires to have His own image reflected so that His goodness can be given in greater measure. He has sent His Spirit of Holiness into you to free you from the things that keep His nature from being revealed in you.

He calls you a "holy nation" born of His Holy Spirit. It is your nature to be holy, just like God. Unknowingly, many people live in opposition to themselves. Although God's holiness dwells within them, they quench the expression of that nature from coming out.

There are many different motives for not sinning. Some do not sin fearing the consequences. Others sin and are always confessing with the attitude that God will forgive them. Then there are those who seldom sin because they have a hatred for sin. The Bible describes the hatred of sin as the fear of the Lord. You need to ask God to develop in you a hatred for sin and then receive it by faith.

This kind of walk before God lifts you into a new dimension of fruitfulness and strength. You have a trust and confidence that God is pleased with you in an ever-increasing way.

Even when you don't feel strong, you can know that the God of all strength dwells within you. Notice Isaiah 40:29-31:

He gives power to the weak, and to those who have no might He increases strength.

Even the youths shall faint and be weary, and the young men shall utterly fall, but those who wait on the Lord shall renew their strength; they shall mount up with wings as eagles, they shall run and not be weary, they shall walk and not faint.

Exchange Your Weakness

In this passage the Lord said that He will give you power and increase your strength as you wait on Him. Waiting does not mean that you sit down passively. It actually means that you bind yourself together with Him by twisting, as a string wrapped around a rope takes on the strength of the rope. When you allow God's Word and nature to be supreme in you and to be expressed through you, you actually exchange your weakness for His strength.

As your life is governed more and more by the Lord and His desires, you not only come to know Him more deeply and intimately, but you find that you more accurately and purely express His compassion and deep desires.

A life pleasing to God—revealing Him—that is our goal and our quest!

CHAPTER 8

Positive Spiritual Progress

The deep, heartfelt desire of God is that His will be expressed in your character and actions. If you are to hear and understand what God is saying clearly, then there must be continual strides toward positive spiritual progress.

First Corinthians 2:9-10 says, "But it is written: 'Eye has not seen, nor ear heard, nor have entered into the heart of man the things which God has prepared for those who love Him.' But God has revealed them to us through His Spirit. For the Spirit searches all things, yes, the deep things of God."

The Holy Spirit is the revealer. Through your sensitivity to His leading and instruction He brings you under His government. His desire is for you to give Him control of your life in a positive manner in order to accomplish two things. First, to bring you into the most satisfying and fulfilling life imaginable—life with a continual flow of peace, stability, and success in your endeavors. Second, to make you into a powerful tool of His love that expresses His desire to bless the lives of others.

Isn't it beautiful to realize that God has a purpose for you? He has prepared such great and wonderful things that you could not even begin to grasp them without His help. God's desire for your progress is so great that the natural mind would not entertain the thoughts of how far God will take you.

Now look at First Corinthians 2:14: "But the natural man does not receive the things of the Spirit, for they are foolishness to him; nor can he know them, because they are spiritually discerned."

Under the Old Covenant, the people could not conceive of these things. But today we have been given the Holy Spirit to reveal them to us. Read verse 10 once again from *The Living Bible*: "But we know about these things because God has sent his Spirit to tell us, and his Spirit searches out and shows us all of God's deepest secrets."

It takes an attitude receptive to the Holy Spirit to understand the things God has provided. And you can open yourself to receive an unveiling of all God's secrets. The adventurous pioneer is not satisfied with his present understanding, but presses on toward deep spiritual achievement.

Many so-called Christian leaders have made inadequate progress, having become content with their spiritual walk. Many believers have settled for immaturity as the norm. Many have lost the zeal for spiritual growth. Maybe they never had it.

After years of a successful ministry and a close relationship with God, the Apostle Paul said, "...Not that I claim to have achieved all this, nor to have reached perfection already. But I keep going on, trying to grasp the purpose for which Christ Jesus grasped me" (Philippians 3:12 *Phillips).*

There are continual and increasing strides for Christ-likeness in every healthy believer. A dissatisfaction with ordinary existence and a pressing on to know God and reflect His nature should dwell within each of us.

Everyone has the potential for progress. God has not been partial, giving one a special ability to progress, and to another the destiny of spiritual immaturity. There is within each one of us the potential ability for tremendous spiritual growth. Anyone has the right to become a giant for God. *You must recognize your potential for progress.*

The way *you* see yourself in Christ sets the boundary for increase in your life. Notice James 1:22-25:

> *But be doers of the word, and not hearers only, deceiving your-selves.*

> *For if anyone is a hearer of the word and not a doer, he is like a man observing his natural face in a mirror; for he observes him-self, goes away, and immedi-ately forgets what kind of man he was.*

> *But he who looks into the per-fect law of liberty and continues in it, and is not a forgetful hearer but a doer of the work, this one will be blessed in what he does.*

The person who begins to see him-self as God sees him unlocks limitless ability in his life. As you begin to truly believe that you are forgiven and pure in God's sight, you realize that you are accepted into the family of God.

You have become an heir of all God's riches. You have been freed from the dominion of sin and death. This is the new "natural man" that you see in the mirror of God's Word.

But too many continue to look at what they are not, instead of what they are. They dwell on their lack and failures. When God reveals the possibilities, they are so cluttered with negativism and ungoverned emotions that they fail to grasp it. If you will change the way you feel about yourself, you will begin to mold your future.

The Perfect Law

The person who looks into this "perfect law of liberty" does not forget what he sees. Instead, he recognizes that freedom belongs to him. He continues to accept God's image of his life rather than his unrenewed thoughts. *The "law of liberty" frees you from the limitations of the old man.*

When the reality of this newness dawns on you, you will grow by leaps and bounds. Because you are created in the likeness and image of God, you have a tremendous capacity for spiritual receptiveness.

When Jesus went up on the mount with Peter, James, and John something dramatic began to take place. The disciples saw the transfiguration of Jesus right before their eyes. He became brilliant with the reflection of the light of God. Through that demonstration we understand two things about mankind. First, you see man's capacity to *receive* the glory of the presence of God. Second, you see the capacity of a man to *reveal* the glory of the presence of God.

When the transforming power of

God entered your life, you received the presence of God. Your true inner-most nature was changed. Your outward expressions began to reflect the inward changes. Your habits, speech, and expressions began to correspond to your true nature.

Tragically, man continues to conform to the old habits, living a masquerade that hides the true nature he received at the new birth. The Bible refers to them as carnally minded. The battle against carnal thinking is everpresent. It is not something you obtain victory over once and for all. Your new way of thinking and living must be maintained daily.

When the flesh is left to direct your thoughts and actions, it will seek to reclaim any lost ground in your life. When your flesh is in control, you are at your weakest point. Leaning toward carnal tendencies and giving in to the demands of the flesh come from habit.

New habits must be formed that put aside those old desires and create the attitudes that promote progress in your life.

> *For if you live according to (the dictates of) the flesh, you will surely die. But if through the power of the (Holy) Spirit you are habitually putting to death— making extinct, deadening—the (evil) deeds prompted by the body, you shall (really and genuinely) live forever. For all who are led by the Spirit of God are sons of God* (Romans 8:13,14 *AMP*).

The word *habitually* means that with the help of the Holy Spirit, you determine to create a new habit. You develop a resistance to the promptings of the body.

Do you remember the shot the dentist gave you that caused the side of your mouth to become numb? There was no feeling on the side of your face because the nerves were deadened. As the habit of following the leadership of the Holy Spirit develops, your spirit will yield to His government, and the flesh will follow as an instrument of service to God. You will be less sensitive to the pull of previous habits. A new sensitivity to the impulses of the Holy Spirit will emerge.

A Burning Desire That Purifies

A burning desire develops within your inner man to be controlled by the Spirit of God just as Jesus was. That burning fire has the same effect on you that fire has on gold: It purifies.

When a goldsmith removes impurity from gold, he heats a small amount of the precious metal until it liquefies. The heat brings the impurities to the surface to be skimmed off. Then the goldsmith can see his own reflection clear and unhindered. Hebrews 12:29 tells us that God is a consuming fire.

As His Spirit moves in your life, He begins to draw you into closer fellowship. The areas that have prevented your spiritual progress will begin to come to light. Not in a condemning way, but with the hope that God will gently skim them from your life in order to allow His reflection to be seen in you. This will require your full cooperation.

The outcome will be a refining of your life and progress toward success in everything you undertake. Isaiah 40:6,7 describes this in such a beautiful way:

> *All flesh is grass, and all its loveliness is like the flower of the field. The grass withers, the flower fades, because the breath of the Lord blows upon it; surely people are like grass.*

As the breath of God blows upon your life, the areas that seemed beyond control will begin to wither and lose strength. But His "breath" will come only with your cooperation and your obedience to God's promptings.

The Condition of the Heart

One very vital key to true spiritual progress is found in the parable of the sower and the seed. In Matthew, chapter 13, Jesus clearly reveals the supreme principle of the Kingdom of God —the principle of "seed planting."

The Word of God is the seed of the kingdom which can produce the will of God in your life. This parable not only reveals the ability of God's Word to produce in you, but it also reveals the importance of the soil. Let's focus on the importance of the soil.

The four types of soil mentioned represent the varied conditions of the human heart. The first type of soil is ground by the wayside, meaning a pathway. It is impenetrable. When the seed of God's Word is planted, it cannot break through because it is hard.

Hard-Hearted Hearers

Many have become hardened for very understandable reasons. Like the pathway, they are hardened because they have been walked on by people. Perhaps it was the abuse of their parents or just one hard knock in life after another. Maybe a failed personal relationship or the rejection from a loved one has let a protective wall develop, preventing anyone from doing such damage again. Whatever the reason, they have built within themselves a resistance to vulnerability.

Though this may be a reason for hardness, it is not an excuse. The destructive effort of this resistance is not only an isolation from people but an insensitivity to God. They have lost the ability to sift out the bad and retain the good. Everything is discarded simply for the sake of protection.

This hardness of heart must be resisted. People will undoubtedly let you down, but you cannot let that sour your feelings toward people. Seeds of God's love will keep you open to people and to God. You must see beyond their failures and refuse to allow your heart to become hardened.

Shallow Hearts

The second type of soil is stony ground, meaning a shallow heart. This is someone who has not allowed the Word of God into his life with any depth. They joyfully receive the promises of God but they have no root. They have never obtained personal confidence in their relationship with the Lord. There is a surface layer of mental assent but no real depth because beneath the façade of spirituality they remain self-centered, untrusting, and unchanged.

These Christians want the results of a life yielded to God, yet refuse to let go of their carnal state of mind. Consequently, they exercise little spiritual power and can do nothing to help their fellowman. Their shallowness prevents the Word from ever truly taking root. When Satan brings trouble into their lives they begin to distrust and abandon the promises of God.

Thorny Hearts

The third kind of soil Jesus calls thorny. This is an overcrowded heart. The seed of God's Word planted in ground cluttered with cares and anxieties will yield no fruit. Within the soil of the overcrowded heart are the weeds of doing-too-much and displaced priorities. As a result, there remains little room for the newly planted seed of God's Word to grow.

It is so easy to innocently become overinvolved with harmless activities. The danger is that you can become so distracted that God's Word has very little priority, thus it has no real effect in your life. They rob you of the time of fellowship and closeness with God. When you are too distracted by projects and duties to spend time alone in fellowship with God, you are too busy!

First Peter 5:7 says, "...casting all your care upon Him, for He cares for you." Cares, anxieties, worries, and concerns fill your mind, distracting you from intimacy with God. They become seed thoughts that will begin to suffocate the Word.

Your inner man will receive whatever seed you plant. The seed you continually sow into your life *will* produce a harvest. Galatians 6:7 from the *Phillips* translation reads: "A man's harvest in life will depend entirely on what he sows."

The seed of the Kingdom of God requires total loyalty. When the pursuits of life steal your loyalty to God's plan, and riches or the pleasures of life become overemphasized, real progress and fulfillment are compromised. The interests we have, the things we obtain, and the pleasure of living must be an expression of our faith in God, not a substitute.

Receptive Hearts

Jesus reserved the best for last. The fourth soil He calls good soil which is the receptive heart. Simply defined, this is someone who hears the Word and is willing to accept any changes needed. This person has a listening heart that pursues understanding.

Because of the attitude of the heart, the seed is planted in healthy soil. There is no hardness, no shallowness, no clutter—only hunger and willingness manifested by a heart yielded to the Spirit of God. King Solomon prayed for an understanding heart (1 Kings 3:9). He later wrote in Proverbs, chapter 2, that an understanding heart was a key to finding the knowledge of God.

When God finds that you have a listening heart, He will begin to plant the seeds of progress in your heart. He will move you from spiritual barrenness into a fruit-producing lifestyle.

Because you hear His voice you will begin to see yourself in a new light. As you walk in that light, more light is given. You become aware of the seeds of health growing within. Seeds of prosperity, progress, and plenty are being nurtured. All of the benefits of a life truly open to God begin to spring up within you.

Receptiveness is a key ingredient for continued progress in the Lord. It will require intense cultivation, but it will result in abounding fruitfulness. It is a sad sight to see scores of Christians wandering aimlessly from one "spiritual fad" to another always wanting to appear mature, yet lacking the common sense to lay the proper foundation for growth.

Develop a Solid Foundation

The Holy Spirit will always emphasize and promote a stable foundation for progress. From this stability He can bring clear direction. He will teach you in a straightforward fashion to deal with the compromise you have tolerated in the past.

The importance of a deep, personal foundation cannot be overemphasized. The development of depth and character must become your priority. Without deep roots in God, some will bear fruit for a time but when the winds of adversity come they will wilt.

Pull together the loose ends in your life. Prayer, study, and tithing must all be a vital part of your new lifestyle. Seek after the fruit of the Spirit and the gifts of the Spirit with the same intensity. Don't be disillusioned—change is required for progress. Let the change come!

Books by Dennis Burke, Ph.D.

*Dreams Really Do Come
True—It Can Happen to You!*

Develop A Winning Attitude

Breaking Financial Barriers

Unleashing Your Potential for Success

You Can Conquer Life's Conflicts

Grace: Power Beyond Your Ability

* How to Meditate God's Word

Knowing God Intimately

The Law of the Wise

* Available in Spanish

For a complete catalog of materials
or to receive a free publication:
Insights: The Way to A New Life
visit our website at:
www.dennisburkeministries.org

Dennis Burke Ministries
PO Box 150043
Arlington, TX 76015
(817) 277-9627

Include your prayer requests.

Dennis Burke is internationally known as a Bible teacher and best-selling author. He has helped thousands of people discover victorious living through faith in God's Word.

Dennis began in ministry as an associate pastor, then moved to Texas to work with Kenneth Copeland Ministries. His involvement with Kenneth Copeland Ministries continues as a guest speaker and contributing author for the *Believer's Voice of Victory* magazine.

Dr. Burke serves as the president of the International Convention of Faith Ministries (ICFM). He is the keynote speaker at churches, conventions, conferences, and retreats worldwide.